Original title:
Succulent Sundays

Copyright © 2025 Creative Arts Management OÜ
All rights reserved.

Author: Rosalie Bradford
ISBN HARDBACK: 978-1-80581-847-2
ISBN PAPERBACK: 978-1-80581-374-3
ISBN EBOOK: 978-1-80581-847-2

Soothing Shades of Weekend Calm

Coffee spills like laughter bright,
A mug that's far from upright.
The plants all giggle in their pots,
As the cat assumes her spots.

With toast that bears a crunchy score,
We dance around the kitchen floor.
Sun beaming in with playful sass,
Who knew weekends could be such a blast?

The Garden's Heartbeat at Dusk

Evening whispers secrets low,
As fireflies put on a show.
The tomatoes blush with pride,
While snails take their sweet time to glide.

Neighbors stare from their porch chairs,
Counting dandelions, catching glares.
As shadows play their cheeky tricks,
The garden hums its twilight mix.

Leisurely Glances at Nature's Canvas

Birds are chirping their silly tunes,
While I munch on leftover prunes.
The flowers wear their brightest hats,
With bees just buzzing 'round like brats.

Sipping lemonade with a grin,
I spot a neighbor's old green bin.
Nature's artwork, wild and free,
Turns every day to jubilee.

Petals Unfurled in Soft Light

Sunrise paints the sky with cheer,
As the garden wakes, we all appear.
Each petal yawns, shakes off the night,
While squirrels race in morning light.

With smiles as wide as grassy lanes,
We laugh at all our silly pains.
Amid the blooms, our hearts take flight,
At play in joy, a pure delight.

Harvesting Dreams Under Clear Skies

In a garden full of chatter,
We pick weeds to make them scatter.
Carrots dance, with smiles so wide,
And rhubarb wants a joyful ride.

Tomatoes wear their polka dots,
While cucumbers lose their pants in plots.
The weather's fine, the sun is bright,
We harvest dreams and share delight.

Warmth of Nature's Abundance

Oh, the berries start to giggle,
As we squish them, oh what a wiggle!
The zucchinis hide behind the beans,
Wishing they could join our scenes.

Lettuce keeps its leafy secrets,
While peas prefer their cozy blankets.
We talk to roots, they're such good friends,
In this quirky place where laughter blends.

Bursting Colors on a Peaceful Day

Peppers blush in red and green,
While eggplants wear their jeweled sheen.
With flowers sprouting, oh so bright,
The sun and veggies share the light.

We're baking bread that smells divine,
With herbs that dance on thyme's design.
Each bite a giggle, each sip a cheer,
Nature's feast is finally here!

Daydreams Among the Ferns

Underneath the leafy green,
We spot a squirrel in between.
He's plotting sneaky nutty schemes,
While we just munch on leafy dreams.

A bunting sings its funny song,
As we sing right along, so wrong!
Fern fronds wave, they join our sway,
In this whimsical garden play.

A Cornucopia of Comfort

On a table piled high with snacks,
A mountain of crumbs, not just a few,
Where laughter bubbles, chatter attacks,
And no one checks if they've had their due.

The dip's too spicy, the chips now fly,
In this game of taste, we're all fools,
Who needs a diet? Oh, why even try?
We munch, we crunch, breaking all the rules.

The Sweet Taste of Slowness

Cinnamon rolls sprawled across the tray,
I just blinked; they've vanished, gone poof!
Morning moves slowly, dreams drift away,
It's a race to the last, so let's get goofed!

Socks mismatched, I stroll in delight,
Coffee spills over, but who even cares?
Time's lost its meaning, but feels just right,
As I savor each sip, life's full of shares.

A Feast for the Senses

Jelly beans scatter, colorful, bright,
Like confetti celebrating our fate,
An endless spread is a wondrous sight,
And taste buds shout, 'Please, load up the plate!'

Beneath the summer sun, we gather round,
Where giggles and crumbs become the best blend,
Every regret of calories unbound,
In this banquet of joy, the laughter won't end.

Daydreams in Juicy Hues

Grapes roll across like tiny green sports,
Each bounce a reminder: I need a snack!
Where juicy dreams reside, our taste buds cavort,
Oh sweetily red, why don't we have a snack?

Melons giggle in the cool summer breeze,
As laughter zips past like light on the ground,
With every slice, we all feel the tease,
Of flavor and fun, where joy is profound.

Serene Sips of Sunday Morn

Coffee spills and giggles rise,
Pajamas stretch, oh what a prize.
Cereal dances in the bowl,
Morning chaos takes its toll.

Toast pops up like it's a game,
Butter slips, it's all the same.
Under blankets, we all hid,
Sunday mornings—oh, what a bid!

Lush Blossoms in Lazy Hours

Flowers sprout where socks don't match,
Dandelions meet a wild scratch.
In the sun, we lay and laugh,
Math's for school, not for this craft.

Bugs join in, it's quite the scene,
They march around like queen and king.
A picnic's planned, but food's all gone,
We feast on crumbs until it's dawn.

The Vibrance of Weekend Whispers

Whispers float on breezy treats,
Muffin crumbs beneath our seats.
Neighbors peek with curious stares,
Laughing loud without a care.

Kites get tangled in the trees,
Crisp air holds all our giggly pleas.
Plans evolve, then take a turn,
The art of chaos: oh, how we learn!

Verdant Vibes on a Sunny Day

Lemonade spills, oh what a splash,
Silly faces, we all dash.
Chasing shadows, running free,
Grass stains come so easily!

Sun hats perched, we pose with flair,
But the selfie fails—grumpy stare.
Still we laugh and dance about,
Weekend's here, without a doubt!

Harvesting Sunday's Delights

Picking berries from my bed,
Pajamas on, no need for dread.
Coffee spills on my shirt, oh well!
Only my cat knows this tale to tell.

Syrup drips on pancakes piled,
My diet plan's been mildly reviled.
Maple's sticky joy and cheer,
My fork's a chariot, never fear!

Vibrant Moments in Leisure

The sun peeks in with lazy rays,
I lounge about, in a daze.
Remote in hand, I flip and flop,
While snacks surround me – never stop!

Mismatched socks on my feet's parade,
Fashion's lost in this escapade.
Each laugh echoes, no rush at all,
As I dive deep in this joyous sprawl.

Nectar of the Restful Hours

A lazy brunch that lasts all day,
Where all the rules just fade away.
Bacon sizzles, friends drop by,
We toast to mornings, oh my, oh my!

Sipping tea in our finest mugs,
By afternoon, we're all just shrugs.
Count the crumbs, we've made a mess,
But who's to judge? We're all blessed!

Bounty of the Weekend Bliss

Oh, the joy of doing naught,
In sweatpants, we just sit and plot.
When dinner calls, we softly groan,
Yet, somehow, we snack like kings on thrones.

In this paradise of lazy fame,
Every hour feels just the same.
With giggles shared and dreams on deck,
Let's clink our cups – oh, what the heck!

The Cusp of Refreshing Change

Sleepy eyes meet morning light,
Coffee brews, it feels just right.
Pajamas on, I dance around,
In my dreams, I shall be crowned.

Chasing socks, a playful game,
Breakfast is my claim to fame.
A pancake tower, oh so tall,
I'll eat it all, or lose it all!

Luscious Layers of Leisure

Weekend vibes, the snacks arrayed,
In my lounge chair, I've delayed.
TV's on, the couch my throne,
I'll conquer snacks, I stand alone.

A sandwich thick, a pickle's plight,
With each bite, I feel the bite.
Friends on board, the couch we share,
Popcorn flying through the air!

Wanderlust in a Jar

A jar of sunshine, pickles stored,
Imagining a trip, I'm bored.
Sand beneath my toes, I sigh,
But first, let's see if I can fly.

Laid-back vibes and snacks galore,
My heart's on sea, my mind's on shore.
Adventures planned for next week's trip,
But for now, I'll just take a sip.

The Serene Symphony of Harvest

Gather 'round, the feast begins,
With each dish, we share our wins.
Lavish bites, the laughter flows,
Who knew food had so many shows?

Pumpkin pies and cornbread dreams,
With every bite, that smile beams.
Autumn's here, let's give a cheer,
More food, more friends, let's persevere!

The Aroma of Sunshine and Leisure

The sun's a chef in the sky's bright dome,
Whipping up laughter, calling us home.
With pancakes stacked as high as the sun,
We giggle and munch, oh, weekend, you're fun!

Birds chirp melodies, a quirky band,
Sipping on juice, feeling quite grand.
Chasing our shadows, we tumble and roll,
In this moment we find our soul's playful goal.

Fragrant Hues in a Calm Horizon

Awake to a canvas of colors so bright,
Smells of fresh laundry drift into the light.
Painted in laughter, our toes in the grass,
Tickling the clouds while we watch the hours pass.

Friends gather 'round, with stories to share,
Wearing mismatched socks, without any care.
We feast on delights, sweets piled in heaps,
Weekends that sparkle, like dreams, never sleeps.

Juicy Joys of the Weekend

Bite into berries, their sweetness divine,
Spinning in circles, it's tasting time!
With watermelon smiles, dripping and sweet,
We dance in the sun, oh, what a treat!

Giggling toddlers, running wild and free,
Sprinklers spraying, like a joyful spree.
As laughter echoes, filling the air,
Who knew this fun was hiding out there?

The Lush Embrace of Daylight

In fields of green where silliness grows,
We dive into sunshine, where nobody knows.
Picnic blankets flapping, a glorious mess,
Sandwiches singing, we bask in the zest.

Time slows down as we trickle with glee,
Juice fights and splatters; we're wild and free.
Underneath the sky, our worries take flight,
In the lush embrace of this spirited light.

The Art of Peaceful Prowess

In gardens bright, where gnomes reside,
They wiggle dance, with arms open wide.
A squirrel chuckles, takes a grand leap,
As flowers gossip, secrets they keep.

Sun-soaked leaves in a jolly parade,
The wind hums tunes, a lively charade.
With coffee cups and hats askew,
Nature smiles, with joy anew.

Embracing Nature's Laughter

A chipmunk mocks a dandy bee,
And makes a dash for the nearest tree.
The petals giggle with every breeze,
Whispering jokes among the leaves.

A clumsy snail gives it a go,
Slipping past a cheerful crow.
With each soft step, the earth absorbs,
The laughter echoing in sweet chords.

Whimsy in the Green Glow

Grapes dressed as planets in bold array,
Inviting laughter to join the play.
While carrots sprout in a jaunty line,
These veggies know how to unwind fine.

Tomatoes blush, oh what a sight!
With jokes ripe as their skins so bright.
The cucumbers dance, in quirky shoes,
Nature's whimsy can't help but amuse.

Morning Dew on Velvet Leaves

Dewdrops sparkle on fuzzy greens,
Like tiny jewels in nature's scenes.
A misty laugh from the dawn's embrace,
As sunlight tickles every face.

A ladybug rolls, gives a sly wink,
While ants brainstorm how to link.
With whispering breezes, giggles ignite,
Morning unfolds with pure delight.

The Plump Pleasures of Time

Oh, the fruits of life we munch,
With every juicy, sweetened crunch.
The clock ticks slow, we laugh and play,
In this delightful, plump buffet.

Bouncing berries, quite the tease,
Sipping nectar like a breeze.
We skip the chores, we forget the grind,
In this joyful feast, true peace we find.

The puddings jiggle, the cakes do sway,
While pies all wink and cats just prey.
A battle with the spoons set in,
Who knew dessert could be a win!

So gather round this table wide,
With friends and treats, let joy be tied.
In whims and giggles, we unwind,
In every morsel, laughter's kind.

Leisure's Luxurious Feast

Let's set the scene with treats galore,
A platter rich we can't ignore.
The cheese wheel rolls, it's on the floor,
Who knew a snack could start a war?

Salads shimmy in colors bright,
While pickles dance with sheer delight.
The breadsticks twirl, oh what a sight,
We munch and laugh into the night.

Whipped cream clouds, they float and gleam,
We dip our spoons and start to dream.
Desserts parade like a grand ballet,
In this feast of fun, we'll laugh away.

The game of crumbs, who's winning now?
With chocolate mustaches, let's take a bow.
In every bite, fine art we weave,
As time stands still, it's hard to leave.

An Oasis of Verdant Calm

In gardens deep where greens abound,
We pluck the herbs straight from the ground.
A melon giggles, ripe with cheer,
Sassy cucumbers, come gather here!

We splash in flavors, fresh and sweet,
The lettuce jokes, oh what a treat!
Mint has a giggle, basil sings,
As nature shares her bustling things.

Tomatoes blush, in flavors bold,
While carrots whisper secrets told.
In this lush patchwork, we explore,
A verdant calm we can't ignore.

Around the picnic, joy's the guest,
Food fights spark and laughter's best.
In this grassy theatre, green and bright,
We frolic in this silly bite!

Nature's Edible Whispers

Nature calls with tasty hints,
Peas play tricks and shallots sprint.
Corn on the cob shows off its flair,
While every veggie spikes the air.

A grape in hand, a silly grin,
Oh, let the munching games begin!
With every crunch, a giggling spree,
As kale just laughs, so wild and free.

Fruits high-five and give a cheer,
While the limes flirt, oh dear, oh dear!
We feast like kings beneath the sun,
In this garden lounge, we laugh and run.

So come and play, the table's set,
With nature's whimsy, no regrets.
In playful whispers, snacks aligned,
A funny feasting of the kind!

Nature's Palette on a Day of Ease

Colors splash across the sky,
A canvas ripe, no need to try.
Birds wear hats, dogs dance a jig,
Even the flowers are feeling big.

Grasshoppers hop in tuxedo vests,
Clovers whisper their silly quests.
Ants march band-style, the picnic spread,
While bees argue over who's the bread.

The sun grins wide, a jolly old chap,
Clouds wear smiles, it's a cushy nap.
Nature chuckles in a playful spree,
Who knew the outdoors could be so free?

Lemonade rivers flow down the hill,
Ice cream trees, oh what a thrill!
It's a day where laughter bubbles bright,
In nature's palette, everything feels right.

Radiant Moments in Gentle Breeze

Wind tickles leaves, a merry tease,
Squirrels strut like they own the trees.
Bees buzz gossip with sassy replies,
While grass grows tall, claiming its prize.

Flip-flops slap, a rhythm divine,
Sun hats wobble, sipping lemonade wine.
Caterpillars sport some stylish attire,
Insects bust moves, taking us higher.

Crisp chips crinkle, a crunch so loud,
Picnic party, we gather in a crowd.
Nature snaps photos, no need for a lens,
Capturing antics of fuzzy old friends.

Laughter like bubbles dances in the air,
Even the clouds can't help but stare.
A day like this, no work to be done,
Spreading joy under the cheeky sun.

Earthly Delights Beneath the Sun

Sandwiches struttin' in layers of cheer,
Potato chips join them, oh dear, oh dear!
Pickles parade in their briny glow,
Who knew lunch could put on a show?

Daisies giggle, swaying their heads,
As toddlers tumble from their grassy beds.
A picnic blanket, a kingdom of fun,
Capping the day like a splendid bun.

Clouds play hide-and-seek with the sun,
Nature runs wild, but oh what fun!
A kite gets tangled in a tree of flair,
The wind, a cheerleader, floats in the air.

Bugs are battling in a silly smackdown,
While ants form a conga line straight to town.
It's a feast of delight, a festival grand,
Together, we thrive, hand in hand.

Refreshing Blooms of Carefree Times

Tulips prance in their colorful dresses,
Dancing for guests who bring tasty guesses.
An old tree laughs at its own slight lean,
Whispers of humor, nature's routine.

The sunbeams giggle, tickling the breeze,
As dandelions blow kisses with ease.
Mirth fills the air as laughter is heard,
It's a nature party, no need for a word.

Cards are shuffled, with the ants as the glee,
Guessing games played, 'What's under that pea?'
Chilly drinks fizz, like laughter unbound,
Each bubble pops happily, swirls around.

In gardens where troubles take a long break,
Humor grows wild, no need for a lake.
Nature's refreshment, oh so divine,
Every moment giggles, it's truly a sign.

The Senses Awakened

Awake with a giggle, the sun yawns wide,
Bacon-scented dreams take us for a ride.
Coffee's aroma wafts through the air,
Even the cats seem caught in the flair.

Pancakes wave flags of syrupy cheer,
Waffles huddle close, bringing sweet frontier.
Laughter erupts as we munch and chime,
Saturdays are silly, perfecting their rhyme.

The toast pops up like a toast at a feast,
Eggs shimmy and shake; it's a breakfast beast.
All senses collide in this frolicking space,
As we gobble the joy, like it's a sweet race.

Sundays steal time with a playful jest,
Where the fridge is a treasure, and breakfasts are best.
With giggles and crunches, we gather around,
In this silly kingdom of flavors, we're crowned.

Toward Whimsy's Embrace

In a land where the pancakes flip high and wide,
We gather our giggles and jump on the ride.
The cereal sings tunes sweet and absurd,
Each spoonful a promise, each crunch a word.

The coffee still grumbles, "I'm brewing with glee!"
As the muffins warm up, they dance with a spree.
With each sunny sip, the laughter inflates,
In this joyful realm, nothing suffocates.

Jams swirl like rainbows atop fluffy bread,
With butter that glimmers, let's paint it all red.
Spoons twirl like ballerinas in motion,
As we bask in the chaos, a breakfast devotion.

Here laughter's the flavor; let's spread it around,
In this whimsical dance, watch the fun unbound.
We train all our senses for flavors to find,
In this whirlwind of joy, let your spirits unwind.

Glorious Arrivals in Green

Here comes a chubby avocado parade,
With limes that do tango, in shades that won't fade.
Fresh basil leaps joyfully, green with delight,
While tomatoes make music, a phenom in sight.

Chickpeas giggle, like thunderclaps bright,
Hummus flows freely, a creamy delight.
Spinach holds court with a leafy grand grin,
As radishes blush, showing cheeks made of skin.

Kale dons a crown made of crisped golden hue,
While peppers hop in, wearing colors anew.
The garlic joins forces, a flavor parade,
In this vibrant arena, where all is displayed.

So lift up your forks, let's dance on the floor,
In a world full of veggies, let's ask for some more.
We'll feast with loud laughter, and joy in between,
In this glorious gathering, forever we glean.

The Breathe of Nature's Kiss

Morning spills laughter in petals and dew,
Nature ignites with a bright, leafy view.
The breeze whispers secrets through trees all aglow,
While butterflies giggle, putting on a show.

The birds put on hats made of finest twine,
Serenading the blooms, with a melody fine.
Ants march in step, like a tiny parade,
On this fine Sunday, no effort is made.

With pizza and salads, we savor each bite,
As sunlight streams in, everything feels right.
Cucumbers chuckle and join in the fun,
Under nature's warm gaze, we bask in the sun.

So let every flavor invite you to play,
With spoons and with laughter, we'll brighten the day.
Inhaling the zest, and the moments we share,
Life blooms with a giggle, love floats in the air.

Ecstasy in the Weight of Shadows

On lazy days we float around,
With chips and dips on solid ground.
A bottle pops, the giggles fly,
As snacks balloon, we laugh and sigh.

The dog's in charge, he's got the meal,
Begging hard for pack's great deal.
While we pretend we just don't see,
The chaos that's our doggie spree.

The sun's a tamale under drapes,
The laughter, it escapes like scrapes.
With puns and jests, we pull a string,
And life, oh life, starts to zing.

So if you join this wacky fuss,
Just bring your snacks and ride the bus.
In shadows cast by laughter's dance,
We'll play the game, and just take a chance.

Gentle Hues of Fulfillment

In pastel tones, we craft our cakes,
With sprinkles bright, and silly shakes.
Each bite a burst, a giggling joke,
As icing drips, and laughter's woke.

We toast to blunders, mischief's flair,
While crumbs and giggles fill the air.
The cat now sports a frosting hat,
As guests all join, in love and spat.

Oh, joy is found in sweet excess,
With every bite our lives impress.
So bring your fork to this grand feast,
For humor here, it never ceased.

With every laugh, we raise a cheer,
And share the joy with those held dear.
Our table's set for fun galore,
In every crumb, there's always more.

Springs of Charm and Whimsy

A garden sprout, with plants galore,
We play and dance, who could ask for more?
With watering cans like laughter's tides,
We splash and play, as sunlight hides.

And weeds become our targets bright,
With pitches wild, a daily fight.
The neighbors stare, we've lost our mind,
Who knew the yard could be so blind?

With pots of clay, we craft our scene,
Like silly shoes, oh what a dream!
We'll plant our jokes, and let them grow,
In every corner, charm will flow.

So hop along this lively spree,
With lilting laughs and joie de vie.
In gardens wide, we find our kicks,
With every bloom, another trick.

The Restorative Splash

With splashes great, we jump and dive,
In pools of fun, we feel alive.
A belly flop, a graceful twirl,
Our Sunday best, in water swirl.

The goggles fog, but still we grin,
As perfect aims become a sin.
A cannonball with all our might,
Creates a wave, a joyful sight.

The sunbeams dance upon our toes,
With giggles high, a summer's prose.
As drinks exchange in breezy play,
We toast to all, our wacky way.

So join the fun, unleashing glee,
In puddles bright, come splash with me.
For laughter's drift will surely last,
In water's joy, we find our cast.

Tranquil Blooms in Golden Rays

In the garden, blooms so bright,
Tiny critters take to flight.
A bee with charm, a bug with flair,
Dance of nature fills the air.

Sunshine laughs as petals play,
Fluffy clouds drift far away.
Ladybugs, they strut with pride,
On this joyride, they'll collide!

Crickets chirp their silly tune,
While flowers sway and twist in June.
Watering can spills some cheer,
As gnomes tease from yonder sphere.

Nature's giggles, what a treat,
With every sprout, a little beat.
Laughter echoes through the leaves,
In this patch where no one grieves.

Whispers of Green in the Afternoon

A cactus wears a silly hat,
Wondering where the daisies sat.
The tomatoes throw a party wide,
As pumpkins roll with joyous pride.

Sunbeams poke the lazy grass,
While frogs in puddles spin and bass.
A breeze comes by, gives flowers a tickle,
While gnomes laugh loud, doing a giggle.

With snack time here, the ants unite,
Heaps of crumbs, quite the sight!
Sassy herbs with funky poses,
Vow to spread their fragrant roses.

In this realm where greens confab,
A lettuce slips into a cab.
What a riot, such a spree,
In this patch of glee and glee!

The Sweetness of Stillness and Growth

Nestled 'neath the orchard's cheer,
An apple grins from ear to ear.
Ripe and ready, but what's the rush?
It knows it's never just a hush.

Carrots giggle in the ground,
Wiggling roots make quite the sound.
Chasing shadows, they weave and twirl,
In deep rich soil, they jump and whirl.

With bees in hats and daisies tall,
Nature's pretense, a grand ball.
Shy violets peek out with pride,
In this crazy garden ride!

Sweet tomatoes play hide and seek,
While radishes poke and peek.
Laughter rings through boughs and vines,
In these sweet curls of nature's signs.

Sunlit Reflections in Nature's Fold

Basking in the sunlit glow,
A dandelion steals the show.
Frolicking leaves, with joy, they shout,
As squirrels dare to dance about.

Snapdragons laugh, with mouths agape,
While butterflies make a colorful cape.
Overhead, the clouds do jest,
As crickets settle for a rest.

Bees in glasses, sipping nectar,
Claiming the prize for best inspector.
Fog rolls in, what's this game?
Flora giggles, it's all the same!

Every bloom has tales to tell,
Jokes spread wide, oh can't you tell?
In this space, all laugh aloud,
Nature's joy, it wears a shroud.

Picnic of Possibilities

A blanket spread on grass so green,
With snacks unseen and ants too keen.
Lemonade spills, what a delight,
We chase our dreams, and maybe a kite.

Kite goes up, snacks take a dive,
Mustard flies, is that a bee hive?
We laugh and gobble, bites all around,
In this picnic, joy can be found.

Seagulls swoop, oh what a tease,
"Do you mind?" I say, "This is cheese!"
The fruit flies in quite a show,
This gathering truly steals the show.

The sun shines bright, with laughter and cheer,
Upside-down cakes announcing their rear.
We lie back, enjoy the spread,
With food and giggles, worries shed.

The Fruitful Pause

On this day, we halt the grind,
With cherries sweet and cookies combined.
Whipped cream clouds dancing on pies,
It's amazing what a little fun buys.

Watermelon spills like summer's art,
Grapes roll away, oh where do they start?
We chase them down with giggling glee,
A slippery race, just you and me.

The fruit bowl's full, like our delight,
One more slice, oh what a sight!
Bananas split, laughter fills the air,
In this sweet pause, we have not a care.

As shadows stretch and sunbeams fade,
Our funny talks linger, never frayed.
Juicy moments, we vow to replay,
In this fruit-filled sun, we'll gladly stay.

Blissful Days of Indulgence

Chocolate fountains cascading high,
With marshmallows floating, oh my, oh my!
Cakes and candies, a sugary dream,
Who knew that joy could burst at the seam?

Sprinkles huddle like party-goers,
Wobbling plates, as laughter showers.
Donuts in rows like a sweet parade,
Where calories don't count, just joy made.

Every bite's a giggle, a laugh to share,
Jellybeans roll, creating a scare.
We taste the rainbow, chase down a slice,
In this delicious chaos, there's nothing precise.

Time ticks slow, as we munch and grin,
Ice cream cones adorned, let the fun begin!
With every bite, a memory flows,
In this blissful haze, friendship grows.

A Garden's Embrace

Among the blooms, the laughter starts,
With veggies dancing, oh how it imparts!
Tomatoes blush as they cheer us on,
While daisies giggle at the break of dawn.

Cucumbers sneak into the fray,
"Not on my salad!" they shout and sway.
Zucchini rolls, oh what a ball,
Together we frolic in this garden's thrall.

Carrots contest, "We're sweet, not shy!"
While radishes yell, "We're spicy, oh my!"
A vegetable feud on this leafy plot,
In this green embrace, joy is always hot.

Petals surround us, nature's light,
As we laugh and munch 'til late at night.
In this garden, our spirits will bloom,
Savoring moments, dispelling all gloom.

Savoring the Splendor

On a lazy day, we feast,
With snacks piled high, a delicious beast.
Laughter echoes, jokes in the air,
Chips in one hand, a drink with flair.

Giggling at crumbs that fall with grace,
Spilling soda all over the place.
Life's a party, no strictures or rules,
We're just a bunch of snack-loving fools.

Winding Paths Through Verdant Delights

In gardens lush, we roam and play,
Chasing butterflies, come what may.
Knocking over gnomes, they can't complain,
For we're the kings of this snack parade.

With sandwiches tossed, and grapes that dart,
It's a culinary race, now that's an art!
Forget the rules, let the chaos reign,
A picnic's not a picnic without a bit of rain.

An Eden of Rest

In our secret nook, we lay and dream,
Sipping lemonade, life's a gleam.
Lizard on a log, giving us the eye,
Who knew reptiles could be our spy?

Relishing each crunch, a veggie's delight,
Until someone yells, 'That's not a bite!'
Diving for chips like a swim in the sea,
The snacks at hand are calling to me!

Sip of the Sweet Life

With fruity drinks that sparkle bright,
We toast to the day, everything feels right.
Swirling straws with a wink and a grin,
Inviting friends to jump right in.

Giggles spill like soda foam,
Creating chaos in our little dome.
Who needs a schedule, with joy we explore,
In this glorious mess, who could ask for more?

Blossom-Crowned Sundays of Serenity

Petals dance on lazy air,
Sipping tea without a care.
Lemon cakes and giggles too,
Honey, where's the cat? Oh, boo!

Daisies peek from bright blue vases,
Frogs jump in with funny faces.
A garden gnome joins with flair,
Leaving footprints everywhere!

Birds are chirping songs of cheer,
But I'm stuck in my comfy chair.
With crumbs all over, I proclaim,
Who needs exercise? It's such a shame!

So let's embrace this joyful breath,
In silliness, we'll find our depth.
With friends and snacks, we take the stage,
Sundays, oh, our playful page!

Vibrant Echoes in the Quiet Bloom

Lilies giggle in the breeze,
While I'm lost in bumblebee tease.
A picnic spread, oh what a sight,
Chocolate stains, oh what a plight!

Sun hats tilted, laughter shared,
Chasing ants, we've all prepared.
Grass stains mark our Sunday best,
As we jest and joke, just like the rest!

Tasting lemonade so divine,
Spilling sugar, oh, it's fine!
A sherbet rainbow on my nose,
This funny day just overflows!

So let the blooms take center stage,
In our laughter, we engage.
Let echoes of joy spiral high,
In this floral symphony, oh my!

Awakened Colors of a Gentle Day

The sun peeks in with a cheeky grin,
As garden gnomes plot their win.
Brick paths lead to muffin towers,
Where we crown ourselves with flowery hours.

Dandelions pop, a golden fleet,
And we dance to a skip-hop beat.
With forks held high, we try our luck,
Our Sunday vibes are all unstuck!

Butterflies flutter, colors wild,
As I munch and act like a child.
Messy faces, smiles so bright,
Chasing daylight till it feels right!

So let's toast to day's delight,
With cake and giggles, oh, what a sight!
In shades of laughter, we will sway,
Embracing joy in every way!

Chasing Shadows in a Floral Retreat

Shadows dance beneath a tree,
But the cookies are calling me!
Rabbits hop with style so grand,
While I'm stuck in cookie land.

Bumbles buzz with tales to share,
As we weave our laughter fair.
Hot cocoa spills, oh, what a mess,
But joy like this? It's truly blessed!

Floral hats, oh what a sight,
A little humor, pure delight.
We'll play tag with daisy chains,
And wrangle up some silly gains!

Let's chase shadows; we don't care,
In our little world, there's magic in the air.
With petals scattered, hearts are free,
In this floral harmony, we'll always be!

Vibrant Tranquility Unfolds

A cactus brought its cousin tea,
While orchids danced a waltz with glee.
Succulents in shades of green so bright,
Claimed the sun, basking in delight.

Laughter bubbled from pots so small,
They shared their secrets, one and all.
Gossip bloomed in every corner,
Causing petals to blush, a little warmer.

The aloe winked, with wisdom rare,
'Take it easy, we've naught to care!'
While ferns were twirling, free as air,
All under sunlight's gentle glare.

As evening fell, they tucked in tight,
Under the stars, they'd sleep tonight.
Dreaming of water, sun, and fun,
Filled with laughter, each one a pun.

Garden Party of Perception

In a pot of soil where dreams arise,
Little greens wear clever guise.
A party's brewing, bring your best,
A succulent feast, we'll never rest.

The jade plant's hat was quite the sight,
Adorning it, a daisy bright.
While the rubber tree showed off its flair,
Swaying to music, lost in air.

'Let's play charades!' a sage did shout,
While others laughed, with jolly clout.
A palm tree posed, pretending to swim,
As cacti chuckled, they joined in grim.

With wormy jokes that left them sore,
Roses throwing shade from way back yore.
Underneath the sun's warm glow,
All danced with joy, the fun did flow.

Colorful Reflections in Stillness

In tiny pots, a bright display,
Cacti chuckled in their own way.
Petals giggling, swaying low,
A kaleidoscope of fun to show.

'Look at me!' a bold chive said,
With a green top hat upon its head.
Succulents traded joking tales,
As gentle breezes made their sails.

A string of pearls rolled off to play,
Tumbling 'round, a soft ballet.
While lilies tried to hold their ground,
As daisies warbled silly sounds.

Reflection pools were filled with fun,
As colors danced, a wobbly run.
In stillness, laughter filled the air,
Nature's jesters without a care.

Earth's Palette of Pleasures

In earthy hues and vibrant tones,
A gathering of greens ignites the bones.
From tiny leaves to those quite wide,
Nature's palette, our joy and pride.

The dragon fruit bore tales of lore,
While succulents plotted pranks galore.
A peppy plant with flowers so bright,
Spun stories 'neath the silver light.

'Let's paint the garden!' a sprout did cry,
With colors that would surely fly.
While sharing seeds of laughter sweet,
In a botanical feat, all could meet.

So raise a glass of dew and cheer,
To every plant that gathered near.
In an earthy palette, bold and true,
We celebrate life, the greenest crew!

The Plush Palette of Pagan Leisure

In a patch of vibrant hues,
The flowers gossip, sipping dew.
They wear their colors bright and bold,
While bees dance 'round, a sight to behold.

Gnomes barbecuing in the sun,
Invite the squirrels for some fun.
With veggie burgers on the grill,
Nature's feast provides the thrill.

A ladybug with swagger walks,
While daisies giggle, sharing talks.
The breeze brings tales, oh what a day!
Where laughter blooms in strange ballet.

Each petal's wink, a cheeky tease,
As butterflies dance with such ease.
In this land of fuzzy charms,
Life is safe in cactus arms.

Sundays Bathed in Color

A rainbow spills across the park,
Chasing shadows until it's dark.
The sun wears shades, looking quite sly,
While clouds compete in a cotton pie.

Daffodils flaunt their yellow glow,
While tulips blush in a floral show.
Trees whisper secrets in the breeze,
As picnic ants gather with ease.

We laugh a lot, perhaps too loud,
While toasting marshmallows to the crowd.
A squirrel steals fries right off my plate,
A thief in nature's grand estate.

Paint splatters when kids run free,
Their laughter echoes, wild as can be.
On Sundays bright, the joy we seek,
In this colorful, cheeky peak.

Refreshing Sips of Serenity

Lemonade flows like endless streams,
Quenching thirsts and sunny dreams.
Ice cubes jingle, a merry tune,
While laughter bubbles up to the moon.

A frog hops by in shades so neat,
Complaints of flies become a treat.
The sun sticks its head out to play,
As funny hats steal hearts away.

Mason jars filled with bright delight,
Prepare our spirits for the night.
With quirky straws and fruity splashes,
Even time slows down and dashes.

On cushions made of grass we rest,
With nature's humor, we feel blessed.
A hummingbird winks, it knows the score,
In this bliss, we crave for more.

Bask in Nature's Freshness

In flip-flops, we stroll through lush blooms,
While butterflies clear out the glooms.
A jester sun plays peek-a-boo,
Tickling toes as it bends in two.

Pine cones tumble, a loony race,
Dandelions tickle each other's face.
We try to catch them but they flee,
With giggles hidden in every tree.

Painted plums dangle, a fruity tease,
While sunflowers wave like beachside breeze.
A scarecrow points out a wandering ant,
Whispering secrets in a funky chant.

So raise a glass to moments bright,
To nature's antics, pure delight.
For in this world of fun and cheer,
Every silly smile deserves a beer!

Daylight's Edible Portrait

In gardens where the chaos sways,
Lettuce giggles, parsley plays.
Tomatoes in a dance, quite bold,
Yelling, "Eat me! I'm worth my weight in gold!"

Cucumbers wear sunglasses, oh so cool,
Radishes join in, breaking every rule.
Carrots are rootin' for their chance to shine,
While cabbage rolls in with a swagger divine.

The Garden's Lyrical Gasp

Beets are blushing, standing in a row,
Whispering secrets to the beans below.
Zucchini dreams of being a star,
While peppers boast of their spicy avatar.

Onions cry jokes, yet no one can tell,
A sharp punchline that rings like a bell.
Herbs are giggling under blue skies,
Basil winks, and the whole garden sighs.

Radiance in Every Bite

All the colors blend, a fruity parade,
Bananas do the cha-cha, finely displayed.
Oranges shout chorus lines so bright,
Mangoes and melons join in for the fight.

Each bite a punchline, sweet humor flows,
In a salad of laughter, where everyone glows.
Desserts with sprinkles make the garden sing,
Joy is the harvest that summer will bring.

The Sweetness of Carefree Hours

Time skips by on watermelon peels,
Lemonade laughter is all that it reveals.
Cookies pretend to be healthy delight,
While ice cream swirls in a frosty flight.

Picnics erupt with a homey charm,
Each bite a burst, like a balmy balm.
Giggling ants steal crumbs from the host,
While fruit flies plan to raid this banquet toast.

Fruitful Moments of Reflection

With grapefruits dancing on the floor,
Lemons giggle, then roll out the door.
Bananas slip on a peel or two,
While berries whisper, 'What shall we brew?'

In this garden of snacks and delight,
Cherries chuckle, their cheeks all bright.
Peaches poised for a pie in the sun,
Say, 'Why walk when we can have fun?'

Pineapples crown the party with glee,
While mangoes decide, 'Let's climb that tree!'
Time to savor this fruity fiesta,
No worries allowed, just joy and jester!

So gather the fruits, let laughter flow,
In this moment, let flavors grow.
Each bite a giggle under the sun,
Fruitful moments where joy's never done.

The Eden of Restful Sips

In a land where coffee beans play dress-up,
Tea leaves waltz, in a whimsical cup.
Milk froths swirl in a dance quite sublime,
As lemon slices join in just in time.

Juices unite for a splash of delight,
With flavors that tickle from morning to night.
Straws like confetti in bright colors sing,
Inviting us all to embrace this fling.

Coconut whispers, 'I'm here for the fun!'
While bubbles in soda pop laugh, 'Let's run!'
A sip of joy in this Eden we've found,
Each drop a giggle, so laughter abound.

So raise up your glasses, let merriment flow,
With every refreshing sip, watch worries go.
This garden of drinks keeps the spirit alive,
In the Eden where funny flavors thrive.

Nature's Rich Repose

Under clouds dressed in cottony fluff,
Sunnies giggle, saying, 'Life's pretty tough!'
Breezes play tag with the dandelion,
While bees buzz around, feeling quite fine.

Trees wear capes of the color green,
Tickling breezes, in a humorous scene.
Grasshoppers leap in a jumpy parade,
As flowers gossip, saying, 'We're made!'

A squirrel drops acorns, oh what a sight,
While rabbits hop, stirring up some delight.
Nature's a stage where strange antics unfold,
With giggles as rich as the blossoms of gold.

So let's frolic where laughter does bloom,
In nature's rich repose, dispelling all gloom.
With a wink from the sun and a nudge from the breeze,
Find joy in the little things—oh, do as you please!

In the Company of Color and Calm

In the garden where colors collide,
Red and yellow play tag, just outside.
Purple plums giggle, 'Let's climb up the wall,'
While oranges tumble, 'We're having a ball!'

Butterflies flit with a delicate grace,
Whispering dreams in this whimsical space.
Flowers are laughing, their petals all bright,
As the sun joins in, painting day into night.

In this company here, where vibrance abounds,
We dance with the colors, with no need for sounds.
A riot of hues, like a palette of cheer,
Inviting us all to forget every fear.

So bring your laughter, your quirks, and your smile,
In the company of calm, let's stay for a while.
For amidst all the fun, there's much to explore,
Where color reigns free, who could ask for more?

Tender Leaves of Tomorrow

In the garden of dreams, I trip and fall,
Crunchy greens calling me, 'Hey, have a ball!'
With veggies in hand and dirt on my face,
I laugh at my antics, a messy embrace.

The spinach is winking, the tomatoes jest,
'Old salad recipes? Now that's a jest!'
Drizzle some dressing, let's make a splash,
Who knew greens could cause such a clash?

Lettuce with jokes, carrots with glee,
They dance on the plate, come join their spree!
Spin the fork, twirl the knife, what a feast,
Even broccoli giggles, it's gone to the east!

So let's toss our cares with laughter and glee,
In this garden of joy, wild and free.
Bring on the flavors, don't hold back your cheer,
Tomorrow's tender leaves will soon disappear!

Morning Dew

Wake up with splashes, the sun's on a roll,
Berries are bouncing, they want to be whole!
I toast to the sunrise, with juice in my hand,
Grooves on my plate, it's breakfast unplanned!

The pancakes are flipping, they've got style and flair,
Syrup is dripping, my taste buds beware!
Waffles conspire, teamed up with an envie,
They grin as I drown them like deep-sea saline!

Coffee's on fire, it's brewing with sass,
Mugs raised by the morning, oh what a class!
My cereal's dancing, it's tapping the beat,
Crunchy and sweet, it's a breakfast treat!

So here's to the dawn with flavors galore,
Each sip and each bite, I couldn't ask for more!
With every sweet drop and every bold brew,
I chuckle and sip, oh, the morning's so new!

A Sweet Embrace

In the warmth of the kitchen, a whiff fills the air,
Cookies are chuckling, they know we're all there!
Flour flies high as I dance on the floor,
Spoons in my hands, let's prepare for more!

Eggs in the bowl sing a scrambled tune,
While sprinkles play hide-and-seek with the spoon.
Chocolate chips whisper, 'We've come to unite,'
They cuddle in dough, what a delicious sight!

Baking's a riot, flour fights take flight,
Laughter erupts, in sweet sugar delight!
Brownies are plotting to steal the show,
With icing so bold, they're ready to glow!

So let's rise to the challenge, bake with a grin,
Life's batter of moments, let's mix in some win!
With howls of delight and treats so divine,
In our sweet embrace, it's fun all the time!

Flavorful Hues of Midday Light

Lunch bowls a laughter, colors collide,
Sandwiches chatting, they're peeking inside!
Avocado's calling, bright green and bold,
With laughter and crunch, it's a tale to be told!

Chips on the side, they practice their cheer,
They ripple with giggles,, who's taking the spear?
Guacamole's ready, it's raring to go,
Together we munch, let the flavors flow!

Salads are vibrant, tossing their gifts,
With dressings of joy, they make tummy shifts.
Tomatoes are plotting, a heist with some spice,
Who knew lunchtime could feel this nice?

So fork in one hand, and fun in the other,
Each bite brings a chuckle, like friends of a mother!
With midday delights, we savor each hue,
Flavorful hues, oh, the joy feels so true!

Blooming Joys of Rested Hearts

As evening descends, the table is set,
With laughter and stories, no room for regret!
Desserts are exploding, like fireworks bright,
Each spoonful a smile, a sweetened delight!

Cheesecakes are giggling, 'We're soft and we're grand!'
Brownies are boasting, 'We're chocolate, understand?'
Ice cream is swirling, it's ready to play,
With cookies on top, it's a jubilant day!

Fruits in a bowl are a colorful show,
Berries and bananas in a joyful row!
Whipped cream is chatting, 'Let's top off the fun!'
With sprinkles of laughter, the day is now done!

So let's raise a glass to the joys we have shared,
With bites of sweet laughter, we know we have dared.
In blooming delights of our rested hearts,
Each morsel of joy, a celebration imparts!

An Abundance of Wonder

In a pot of greens, I found a treasure,
Plucking leaves with utmost pleasure.
My cat, confused, gives me a glare,
As I dance in the kitchen, without a care.

A sprout winks as I reach for spice,
Telling me, 'Add more—oh, so nice!'
In this garden of laughs, all feels right,
Like socks on my hands in delight.

The veggies giggle when I prepare,
Whispers of joy fill the air.
Tomatoes blushing in the sun's glow,
They know they're destined for my show.

And as I serve with a flourish and grin,
The feast begins, let the fun spin!
With every bite, a chuckle does bloom,
In the pot, a party, in the room!

The Lushness of Peaceful Time

In the morning light, I find my groove,
A smoothie blend, the blender moves.
Strawberries dance, chocolate chips leap,
In a whirl of bliss, my joy runs deep.

Sipping slow, I taste the cheer,
Mango winks, and I shout, 'Oh dear!'
Papaya plays the joker's role,
Creating giggles that fill my soul.

Friends gather round for a quick taste,
Laughter erupts, no moment to waste.
As we sip from our vibrant bowls,
A joyful ruckus, brightens our souls.

The sun sets low, smiles are wide,
With every sip, love cannot hide.
Chasing flavors with silly pranks,
We toast to bliss, in gratitude, thanks!

Flair of Nature's Palette

In the garden bright, colors bloom,
Chasing butterflies in the afternoon.
Radishes blush, with beets by their side,
Their playful antics, a laugh, we can't hide.

Brushes dipped in fresh-cut thyme,
I paint my plate, it's art, so sublime.
Zucchini noodles dance like they're free,
With every twirl, they giggle with glee.

Dandelions smile, a spark in their eyes,
As I make a salad that's fit for the skies.
Mixing joy with sprinkles of care,
Who knew lunch could be such a fair?

In the crunch and the munch, we all unite,
With veggies in hand, everything feels right.
Each bite bursts forth with laughter and cheer,
In nature's wonder, we hold it dear!

Stillness in Every Sip

With my teacup high, I take a sip,
The chamomile whispers, 'Come take a trip.'
Inhale the calm, feel the cozy hug,
A frog near my feet is giving a shrug.

Sipping slowly, I ponder the day,
And contemplate life in a giggly way.
The kettle sings a sweet old song,
While biscuits tease with their legs so long.

A spoonful of honey takes a leap,
Plopping in the cup, making promises deep.
With every swirl, I chuckle and sigh,
That warm hug in a mug can make me fly.

In this little moment, all feels so grand,
With flavors that tickle, like a magic wand.
So here's to quiet, with laughs that we keep,
In every warm sip, oh blissful leap!

Ripe Reflections of Time

In pajamas all day, what a sight,
My fridge is my throne, pure delight.
Sharing snacks with my loyal cat,
He judges my choices, isn't that fat?

Binge-watching shows, with chips in hand,
Gladly ignoring my workout plan.
The couch is my ship, navigating dreams,
Captain of laziness, or so it seems.

Time flies on by, I'm lost in a daze,
Pondering life in this crunchy haze.
The clock ticks and tocks, but who really cares?
A nap on the couch? Oh, how it compares!

Reflecting on choices from yesterday's feast,
Should I have tried that new recipe beast?
Instead, I embrace my comfy retreat,
For laughter and joy are the best things to eat!

The Taste of a Day Well-Spent

A breakfast of donuts, a lunch full of fries,
Coffee in hand, it's a feast for the eyes.
Dinner's on hold; let's order a pie,
My taste buds rejoice, oh my, oh my!

Each snack is a treasure, a silly delight,
My friends all agree, it's a maxed-out night.
Pizza on plates while we joke and we laugh,
This banquet of joy? Just call it my path.

We sip fancy drinks, with umbrellas so bright,
Toast to our lives, with laughter in sight.
Stories recounted, we roll on the floor,
How did we eat so much? Please, just one more!

As day turns to night, our bellies now full,
The taste of good times is truly a pull.
With memories made, we call it a win,
Here's to tomorrow, let the feast begin!

Vitality in Leisure's Embrace

Awake with the sun and not a care in sight,
Brunch with odd pancakes, oh what a delight!
Flipping them over, a dance of the spatula,
Time stands still, why rush? The day's a dracula.

Laughter erupts between bites of toast,
Each moment we share, I cherish the most.
Sipping on juice, we swap silly tales,
Who knew that relaxation could prevail?

Gardens of laughter bloom all around,
We squabble over who's the best clown found.
The sun shines down, as we sunbathe like whales,
A hilarious sight, here our weirdness hails.

Singing loud songs, off-key and unplanned,
Who knew laziness could be so grand?
With smiles so wide and snacks everywhere,
This primo existence, we breathe in the air!

Infinite Shades of Relaxation

Colors of relaxation dance in the air,
Socks mismatched, who needs to care?
A lazy lounge lizard, I've earned my degree,
In the art of doing nothing, just let me be!

Each couch cushion whispers a soft, warm plea,
'Come rest your head, oh just be free!'
With popcorn in hand, laughter fills the place,
These shades of pure fun always leave a trace.

Chatting with friends, or my favorite show,
Living the life, feeling the glow.
Pajamas all day, life's wild little tricks,
Embrace these moments, laughter's the fix!

As the sun starts to set, in this joyful retreat,
Our spirits ignite, oh what a treat!
With hearts full of joy, we cheer and we sway,
Infinite colors of laughter on display!

Sweet Retreat into Vibrancy

In a hammock, I sway with glee,
While bees and ants plot a party spree.
Sipping lemonade, a sticky delight,
I laugh as my ice cream takes flight!

The cat joins in, with a leap and a bound,
Chasing the sun, oh where can he be found?
Our snack time dance, a comical sight,
As crumbs spread joy, oh what a delight!

Laughter erupts with every new game,
As I toss my hat, it's never the same.
Friends gather 'round in this sunny glow,
With tales of mischief and laughter to flow!

The day slips away, but oh what a thrill,
With silly moments that time cannot kill.
As stars twinkle in the vast evening sky,
I smile at the memories, with a goofy sigh!

Abundance Awaits in Stillness

Nestled in grass, I find my new throne,
Fruits of the season, their sweetness well known.
A picnic spread on this lush green field,
Where tastes and giggles are brilliantly revealed.

Squirrels scurry, plotting their heist,
As I munch on snacks, oh what a feast!
I toss them crumbs, a generous host,
Hoping to win this tree-climbing ghost.

My sandwich escapes, it's peanut butter's fault,
Flew in the air, like a dinner catapult!
We laugh so hard, tears fill our eyes,
As I wave bye-bye to my lunch in the skies!

With laughter ringing and joy in the air,
A roasted marshmallow becomes my sweet wear.
As day turns to dusk, we make silly plans,
To return for more antics with our sticky hands!

Dip into Daylight's Bounty

Under the sun, with a mouthful of cake,
The world looks lovely, or is it a mistake?
Giggles escape as frosting takes flight,
Baking becomes war, a floury delight!

I wear a doughnut like a crown on my head,
As friends roll their eyes at the crumbs I shed.
We skip through a field, twirling with dreams,
Chasing down butterflies, or so it seems!

Chillin' by the pool, cannonballs in play,
As water splashes high in a glorious spray.
I slip and I slide, like a fish on display,
Our laughter erupts, brightening the day!

With a scoop of ice cream that rivals the sun,
Each flavor's a joke, each bite is pure fun.
As the day fades away, we dance in delight,
Shouting "Here's to tomorrow!" beneath the moonlight!

Summer's Embrace in Stillness

In the garden, sunflowers nod and cheer,
As the wind whispers, summer's finally here.
With laughter and games, we bask in the glow,
As the neighbors peek in, they enjoy the show!

I chase after bubbles, floating like dreams,
While my dog runs off, or so it seems.
He tramples the picnic, it's quite a grand heist,
Stealing the sandwiches—oh, isn't that nice!

With lemonade jugs and a karaoke spree,
We belt out tunes, each voice full of glee.
Our dance moves are silly, our joy knows no bounds,
As we twirl and we slip on our funny dance grounds!

Under the stars, we roast marshmallows fair,
With chocolate and laughter filling the air.
We toast to the moments, so carefree and bright,
In summer's embrace, everything feels right!

A Medley of Tranquil Vitality

In the garden, plants gather round,
Filling the air with a silvery sound.
Sipping on sunlight, wearing their glee,
Maybe they're happier than you or me.

Cacti debate who's prickliest here,
Succulents giggle, no reason to fear.
While daisies roll over, making a scene,
Nature's alive, it's a botanical dream.

But one rogue anteater, with a hat that's too wide,
Sneaks in for a nibble, cannot abide.
He dribbles his lunch, oh what a sight,
As these plants chuckle under the sunlight.

So come join the fun, don't be a bore,
These garden shenanigans always bring more.
With greens all around, it's laughter and cheer,
Plant pals unite—let's all grab a beer!

The Comfort of Abundance

Whimsical carrots in a row,
Catch a glimpse of the potatoes below.
Bok choy and lettuce, a leafy parade,
I swear they play games while I'm in the shade.

Tomatoes all blushing in red,
Wondering if they'll go well on bread.
Sweet peppers gossip in colors so bright,
Sharing their secrets all day and all night.

Then comes a bunny, with eyes like a star,
Popping in quickly from way over far.
"Is there enough to share?" he asks with delight,
As veggies unite in a feast, what a sight!

So gather your friends for a culinary show,
Let's sip from the garden, oh what a flow!
With laughter and munching and joy so immense,
The comfort of abundance is simply intense.

Palette of the Daydreamer

Brush strokes of green and splashes of flair,
Each plant a painting, its scent fills the air.
Let's mix colors, oh vibrant and bright,
In this world of foliage, it's pure delight!

Lavender clouds float above laughter,
While marigolds giggle, could they be the master?
The daisies dance lightly, twirling with ease,
As honeybees hum, oh such sweet melodies!

One dreamy tortoise thinks he can fly,
With a dandelion scarf, gives it a try.
But he lands in a patch of soft, fluffy thyme,
And everyone cheers, "Now that's how to climb!"

So let's paint our moments in colors so grand,
With laughter and joy, we'll brighten this land.
In gardens alive with a whimsical tune,
Every inch of this canvas is perfect by noon!

Revel in Nature's Canvas

Every leaf is a giggle, every branch a cheer,
Blossoms are laughing, they've nothing to fear.
In this splendid theatre of nature's own make,
The daisies do pratfalls, just for a break.

Roses declare, "Let's start a dance!"
As violets join in, oh what a chance!
Tulips are twirling in fast-paced spins,
In wild celebration, where everyone wins.

But watch out for squirrels with acorns galore,
They hoard all their treasures, it's a foodie score!
Chasing each other with a nutty delight,
In this festival of flora, it's pure, pure light!

So come take a seat, you're invited today,
To this nature-made party where plants come to play.
With giggles and wiggles and flowers that sway,
Revel in the canvas, let's laugh and display!

www.ingramcontent.com/pod-product-compliance
Lightning Source LLC
Chambersburg PA
CBHW050304120526
44590CB00016B/2482